LAZY LAMA LOOKS AT

Relaxing in Natural Awareness

RINGU TULKU RINPOCHE

Number 6 in the Lazy Lama series

Bodhicharya
PUBLICATIONS
Awaken the heart by opening the mind

First Published in 2015 by
Bodhicharya Publications
24 Chester Street, Oxford, OX4 1SN, United Kingdom.
www.bodhicharya.org   email: publications@bodhicharya.org

ISBN 978-0-9576398-6-7

First Edition. 2015.

Edited by Conrad Harvey, Jonathan Clewley & Mary Heneghan,
from original transcripts by Conrad Harvey,
Maria Hundörf-Kaiser & Carole McMeckan.

Typesetting & Design by Paul O'Connor at Judo Design, Ireland.

Printed on recycled paper by Imprint Digital, Devon, UK.

Cover Image: PeskyMonkey at iStock
Internal illustrations: Conrad Harvey
Lazy Lama logo: Conrad Harvey & Rebecca O'Connor

Editor's Preface

This is the sixth booklet in the Lazy Lama series, in which Ringu Tulku Rinpoche discusses how to relax into realisation, and experience the true nature of mind. It draws on teachings given in Europe over the course of a 12 year period, particularly those at: Dzogchen Beara, West Cork, in January 1994; Conway Hall, London, in 2005; Kagyu Samye Ling Monastery and Tibetan Centre, Eskdalemuir, in April 2006; and St Marks Unitarian Church, Edinburgh, in May 2006.

Conrad Harvey
2015

Contents

Introduction

Buddhism is a path, not purely a belief system. It is a practical way of training ourselves how to feel and experience in a way that reduces our suffering, and increases our happiness.

We don't want pain. We don't want suffering. We want to avoid the causes of suffering. Ideally, we want satisfaction, contentment and happiness. And not just for a short time. We want lasting happiness. The trouble is that we can't remove or avoid everything that might cause us problems. We will become sick. We will become old. And we will die. We will lose what we want to keep. We will encounter what we want to avoid.

We can't clear a lifelong path free of problems, but we can transform the way we experience and react to things. This is where practice comes in.

How we are experiencing right now is a

reflection of our habitual tendencies. On one level we can change our conscious attitude towards things. We can learn that our way of reacting is unhelpful. That it is dualistic and leads to suffering. So, one approach is to work with the situation at a conscious level. The first section of this booklet looks at this approach.

The second, deeper, level is not purely at a conscious level. We need to work at this more subtle level if we want to change our way of reacting. Because, the problem is, we don't choose our emotions. They just happen. Our ways of reacting could be called our habitual tendencies. This is why meditation is necessary, so that we can get to the deepest levels of consciousness. If we're in touch with these levels, then we can have some control over our habitual reactions. So, the second section of this booklet looks at how, in a relaxed and practical way, to transform our way of reacting.

Part I: Opening up to our true nature

Buddhism is about helping people to open up to their true nature. Our true nature isn't being disturbed or unhappy. If it were, we'd be content in those states of mind and would be satisfied feeling miserable. Rather, our true nature is peaceful, compassionate and joyful. And feeling relaxed in that.

In Buddhism, we believe that every being can become awakened. Awakened from ignorance, from all the problems and sufferings of our life. This is possible because the pristine, real, essential true nature of our mind is actually already present. We may not have realised it, but it is there. It isn't diluted or flawed, impure or bad, ignorant or dark. Our true nature is very pure.

You might ask: 'Where is the proof that our mind's essential true nature is pure?

That there's nothing we have to seek from elsewhere, and that we don't have to depend on outside conditions and influences for?'. Well, if we look at our mind at this very moment, when we are not enlightened, even now we can get the proof that the nature of our mind is pure. We just have to look at our mind's nature from three different angles, to see three different qualities.

The three qualities of the true nature of mind

First look: Where is this mind? Is it inside our body or outside? If it is inside, where exactly does it reside? We might answer that neuroscience believes that the mind resides in the brain, but the point here is for us to look at our mind directly from our own experience, in the here and now.

What colour is the mind? Whatever is its shape? If it doesn't have a colour or a shape or anything we can pinpoint, is it there?

If we look for it, we do not find it. It is something we can't get a hold of, locate or exactly define. This thing we call our mind. Therefore, since we can find nothing concrete, we say that our mind's nature is *empty* [see Part II: *'Realising wisdom: emptiness and interdependence'*].

But that is not all. It is not that we just cannot find it, but there's a second aspect to our mind: its *clarity*. Although we cannot exactly say where the mind is, or pinpoint its location on looking at it, we do know that it is there. Although we may not know where it is, or be able to say what it is, we can feel with our mind, see with our mind. We can experience. This is possible because our mind is so very *clear*. So we say that the mind has innate clarity.

There is also a third quality: which we could call mind's *continual flow*. The mind does not stop functioning. Because of its *emptiness* and its *clarity*, its awareness always goes on. All the different kinds of activity and manifestations of the mind, including our senses, never stop. Even when we're asleep our mind is active.

We say that these three are not different, separate things, but the three qualities of one mind. This is what we call the nature of mind: its *emptiness, clarity* and *continual flow* or *unimpededness*.

We can become fully enlightened if we can completely understand these three qualities of mind not just conceptually, but through our own personal experience.

Dualism

So many different kinds of problems in our life come from us not personally realising this true nature of our mind. But, if we can look at our mind, even in this very moment, when we may not be enlightened, we can see how we can become enlightened. This is because the true nature of our mind is not something mysterious or special; the true nature is always right here with us. We just have to experience it.

We experience thoughts and emotions. We can call these manifestations of our mind. It is when we don't understand these manifestations of our mind as purely being just our own manifestations, that the problems start. We get expectations. We get fear. And when our expectations and fear take over, we start thinking and reacting in a way Buddhism calls dualistic. We start to feel that *'this'* is me or mine and *'that'* isn't. We split the manifestations of our mind into two: self and other. And when we start experiencing through this dualism, we create the principal mind poison in our life, which we call ignorance.

So, we are constantly misinterpreting the continuous clarity and flow of our manifesting mind, which we experience as thoughts and emotions, in a dualistic way. This then leads onto suffering, a suffering which is due to just misinterpreting the natural manifestations of our mind.

But if we can recognise the true nature of our mind without this dualism, then we can experience our awakened mind.

Awakening from sleep

The seed of this awakened mind is what we call our true nature or *buddha-nature*. We believe that *buddha-nature* is not only present in every human being, but is present in every being. But most of the time, due to the ignorance we just described, we are just asleep. We don't fully realise who we are.

If we can awaken from this sleep we can become a Buddha, literally '*one who knows*', an enlightened being. Any man, woman or any being, can become a Buddha. To become

JOHN EMBARRASSED EVERYONE
BY BECOMING ENLIGHTENED
ON THE WAY HOME.

a Buddha is not something we have to get, or have to gain from outside – we just have to uncover what is already there and realise our own true nature.

When you become a Buddha and become enlightened, you no longer have a dualistic mind. You do not make a false separation between self and other. You don't have any negative emotions, hatred or jealousy, because all of these are based upon ignorance. These mind poisons are gone. People sometimes misunderstand enlightenment as being spaced out or magically transforming into something immaterial like space – but that is not it at all.

In our unenlightened state we continually have thoughts and emotions arising – the manifestations of the mind. It is said that we still have this same energy when we become enlightened – but the difference is that before we realise enlightenment, our thoughts and emotions are under the control of ignorance. This ignorance means that aversion and attachment, which we could also call fear and desire, then arise.

Mind poisons and karma

It is said that from these three main mind poisons (ignorance, aversion and attachment) all the other negative emotions arise – like anger, arrogance, pride, and jealousy. These negative emotions create a strong impression in our mind, which we call habitual tendencies – the pattern of how our mind functions and experiences from day to day. This pattern is what is called *karma*.

Karma actually means 'action'. An action that we create out of this basic misunderstanding then goes on to create another action. This continuation of action and reaction, on and on, again and again, is what we call *karma*. What we are now, is because of our actions of the *past*. What we will be in the *future*, will be according to our actions in the *present*.

The law of karma is not something very mysterious and very difficult to understand. It is more or less the pattern of our mind. It is our way of looking and our attitudes which have formed in a certain way, and when these continue as a habit we call them the habitual tendencies of our mind.

Getting rid of ignorance

We think of ourselves as something we are not. When our basic understanding is wrong, all of our subsequent beliefs that we create based upon this wrong understanding are also wrong. So difficulties continually arise. We can never put an end to suffering based on this flawed misunderstanding. We can try to solve or avoid problems all the time in life and try to find lasting happiness, but we never find it because our whole belief system is based upon a complete misunderstanding, on a foundation of ignorance.

As long as that ignorance is there we can never completely get to the bottom of all our problems. When one problem is solved, another one pops up. Then another one comes along. All because even the basic nature of how we try to solve the problem is wrong from the beginning.

The focus of Dharma, the teachings of Buddhism, is to go right to the source of this problem, ignorance, the foundation of suffering; to clarify the misunderstanding once and for all. If we can clear this misunderstanding, then we become enlightened. Maybe not immediately, but eventually. It is said that when we become enlightened nothing changes, only our way of looking at things changes, and from that clear view all our problems are solved.

Some people choose to practise Buddhism to get some peace of mind. That is okay, it can help peace of mind. Some people practise to get rid of certain tensions, certain diseases, certain mental problems, that also can be done.

But the most important, main point, the real target and real purpose of practising Dharma is to get rid of ignorance, the basic misunderstanding by which we have all the problems in the first place.

When we get rid of ignorance and come to the right understanding, we call it *'Right View'*. And when the right view is developed through meditation, we become used to the understanding of right view. Our habitual misunderstanding, which we have experienced all our lives, changes, and we experience the right attitude automatically. Then we can become an enlightened being.

Misinterpreting manifestations and fake identities

We cannot find the mind when we look for it. There is nothing we can grasp onto or pinpoint. There is no kind of substance. No independent solid thing. So therefore even when mind is manifesting with thoughts, ideas and emotions, we still say that its basic nature is empty. This is how our mind can manifest in any form and any way; there is nothing which cannot come up in our mind.

If our mind were not empty in nature, it would just be one concrete fixed thing. If that was the case, how could our mind manifest endlessly in the countless and limitless ways we experience every day?

The mind flows; we say that it is *unimpeded* in its nature; it doesn't stop; this is its *continual flow*. But we assume that there is something solid there and we try to grasp at it. We see the mind's manifestations – thoughts, feelings and emotions – and assume there is something independently there, an independent identity which we call *'me,'* and which we could call our ego. That is where we make the basic mistake.

The nature of the mind's *emptiness, clarity* and *continual flow* is actually all the same. But when it manifests we have the habit of misinterpreting it. When the manifestations of the mind (such as thoughts) arise, we start making distinctions like *'this'* is here and *'that'* is there. Because we can see something, we can feel something, then we think that 'I must be *here*; others must be *there*.' We create a dualistic way of looking at our experience.

We lose touch with how our mind is actually flowing all the time, like a river. There is only the fleeting, continuous flow of unsubstantial manifestations. Instead of letting our experience flow in its natural way, we try to grasp and cling to an identity. We perceive things with dualism. We habitually make the wrong decision and try to grasp at something, where there is actually nothing solid or fixed to grasp onto.

Because there is nothing substantial to grasp onto, and everything is always changing, we get afraid that we are losing something. This fear drives us to all kinds of dualistic thoughts. We say 'I can't get my wishes done because of this, because of that.' Then we get frustrated, and we blame others.

Because we do not want change, we try to create something on our own: an identity. Because we have built this identity with our wrong dualistic view, it is very insubstantial and it cannot be maintained. And yet we try to maintain it, and protect it, at all costs.

Our basic nature, as human beings, or as animals, is that we are always looking for appreciation, for recognition, because that helps us to validate our identity. It reassures us: 'If I am acknowledged, I must be here.' It reinforces our misunderstanding, which is a basic misunderstanding, of fixed solidity. This is ignorance, according to Buddhism, because it is a basic way of misunderstanding that is not in accordance with our true nature.

Ignorance can be of two different kinds: either that we know nothing about something; or that we do have an idea about it, but that it is totally the wrong idea. We say that this second type of ignorance, where our (mis) understanding relies upon basically the wrong idea, is the root cause of all the suffering in our world.

How? Well, according to Buddhism, this ignorance creates mind poisons (called kleshas in Sanskrit), the negative or disturbing emotions. We become attached to our identity, and if we have a suspicion that anybody or anything is going to harm or threaten this identity, then we immediately get angry, we hate it. We're attached to keeping this identity and averse to losing it, even though it is empty of any fixed, solid existence.

Impermanence: why suffer?

When we talk about something being empty, it is important not to misunderstand. We shouldn't think: 'We don't have to care for anything. Oh, you know, it is all emptiness'. That would be a complete misunderstanding. We should not just look at our minds and not care for anything else, ignoring our whole environment and whatever is going on. It is important, because if everything is peaceful and harmonious, it makes for a nicer and easier life for ourselves and other beings.

The problem is our usual way of thinking. We think that sorting out all our external problems is the way to happiness and how to be happy. We chase after acquiring nice and pleasant things, and try to avoid what is unpleasant. We mistakenly believe that if we avoid anything unwanted we'll eventually become happy and completely satisfied.

But, if we're continually doing that, we find that we never achieve lasting happiness, we are never finally satisfied, because there's no end to it. It is not as if it can all be sorted out on one day and then it is finished. It becomes our constant way of reacting in life. So if we are constantly reacting like that, how can we be happy and peaceful, because we are always dissatisfied? Either we are trying to avoid something or running after something. So we need to learn how to not react in this way. But this is not easy, as we don't know any other way, because we have done that all our lives. We've always been trying to obtain or avoid something.

One solution is to see that all experiences are fleeting and temporary. What we are experiencing right here, right now, in the next moment has now gone. All the experiences of all our senses are constantly changing, from moment to moment. This moment of my thoughts, this moment of my perception, this moment of my sensation, this moment of my emotion, has now just changed. It is all temporary and impermanent, changing all the time. I'm happy now, but I might be unhappy in the next moment. Our thoughts, emotions, feelings and reactions are all like that.

Therefore, if it is like that – so temporary, with everything changing moment after moment – why should we care so much about it? Why should we so determinedly fight to avoid an experience, which we know is not going to last anyway? Why should we strive to gain something, which we know is not going to last anyway? When all thoughts, all emotions, all sensations, all perceptions are constantly changing and impermanent. Not only them, but I myself am like that too. It is because I am not fixed, but am always changing, that all these things are changing too.

We can learn how to experience things in a way so that, whatever we encounter and whatever comes, it is okay. If a nice thing comes, good, it is very nice, but we don't have to run after it, it is okay. If a not very nice thing comes along, it is also okay, we don't have to run away or fight against it. If we can react in this way, then we will be fine all the time.

But how do we do this?

Part II: Relaxing into realisation

We have described the true nature of our mind, its qualities and how suffering arises from ignorance, attachment and aversion. But Buddhism is a path, not just a philosophy or a belief system. So how do we travel this path and actually develop experience and personal realisation of this true nature of mind? Now we will look at how to go about it.

Understanding and practice: the two wings of a bird

Understanding is vital from the Buddhist point of view, because if we don't have the basic understanding, we don't have the basic kind of background. But then, just an intellectual understanding doesn't completely help us, because just an intellectual understanding doesn't change our way of reacting. So therefore we have to work on our reactions in a practical way.

When we say 'practical', we mean managing our own emotions and reactions from within. For that we use meditation. We could say this is a practical skill, like driving a car. Driving the car is the practical thing. Whereas learning about driving a car is the theory, an intellectual thing. We start the car by turning the key in the ignition. We change gear and put our foot on the accelerator. The car goes and then we turn whichever way we want to go. When we want to stop we just press the brake and that's it – that's the theory. Very easy to learn, we could learn all that for the first time in one minute. Someone could show us: this is the clutch, this is the accelerator and this is the brake and this is the gearstick. But it doesn't mean we know how to drive for real.

If we have to really learn something, then it is not easy, it is more difficult, because it is practical. It involves learning how to do things that we have not been doing before. But it is only by actually doing meditation practice that we can transform our view and experience our true nature.

Meditation

So what is it then? How do you do this 'meditation'? We can describe the theory and how to practise; but then we actually need to do it. The thing is that the theory is very simple: It is that you relax. Relax! It is very easy to say 'relax', but not that easy to do it. I found this out myself, when I was trying to learn how to swim.

I went to Barcelona where the sea is warm. People took me to the beach. So I said 'I must learn how to swim, it looks so nice'. So they said 'Okay, we'll teach you'. They all did. Many people volunteered to teach me, I think about ten people were teaching me. But

I always sank. I first thought that maybe it was my head being too heavy, because I have a big head. My head seemed to sink first, whatever I did. But then they said 'No it is not like that! You just have to relax! Just relax.' I had been doing all sorts of things: people had given me all sorts of exercises. Feet and hands flapping up and down. Breathing in. Breathing out. Nothing had worked. When at last, they'd said 'just relax', I said to myself: 'OK – I have to relax'. And then to my greatest surprise, I found myself floating. That was a fantastic experience, better than when I walked in the Himalayas. I found myself floating. Even my head!

That is what relaxing is, letting go. But it is not always easy.

I probably should say that I can float, as long as I know that I can touch the ground. As soon as I know that I cannot touch the ground with my feet, I sink, because of fear. I can swim very well when I know I can touch the ground.

That is the way we react. So, it is not that I cannot swim, I can swim, but as soon as I have fear, I sink. I think that goes for lots of things.

So relaxing is not always an easy thing. It needs practice, and it is a very important thing to practise.

Our main practice is actually our daily lives. In Buddhism we talk about the Eightfold Path that leads to cessation of all suffering. The Path is defined as Right View, Right Thought, Right Speech, Right Action, Right Livelihood, Right Mindfulness, Right Effort and Right Meditation. Only one of the eight is meditation. Seven out of the eight focus on our daily life. So, we take ourselves and our daily life as the practice.

The main tool is relaxation. We try to apply it to our thoughts and emotions, with gentle mindfulness. We cannot force it. The basic instruction is to be aware. Appreciate yourself. If you note faults within yourself just let go, don't hold onto them.

Just relax

If you don't know how to practise, it is like rock climbing without fingers. Just knowing conceptually is insufficient – whatever you know, what you learn has to be applied practically.

One way to relax is with calm-abiding meditation (In Tibetan it is called *shiné*, in Sanskrit it is called *shamatha*). The purpose is to allow the mind to calm down, to allow it to be still. When our mind becomes stable, becomes still, then our mind becomes clear. Then the tension, the turbulence that is stirring up our emotions and our different kinds of thoughts, cools down, so now we can see clearly, we can think clearly. We are actually purifying the different turbulences of our mind: the negative ways that take over our mind and lead us wherever they like.

We have disturbance as a habitual tendency – a state of mind that's not easy to change and which is based on many layers of assumption. You could say we're like cabbages we have to peel away the layers...

Oi! Who You Callin' a Cabbage?

To be aware of our natural state of mind we have to learn to be natural: we have to learn to be at peace; to observe without reacting with aversion or attachment. We sometimes call the state of mind that's always running away or running after things the monkey mind.

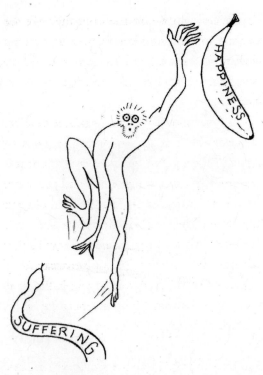

We end up feeling exhausted by constantly investing time and energy into unhelpful things, obsessing over trivia and ruminating over countless possibilities.

So, how do we do the opposite? We are so used to running away from, and running after, things that we have to learn to relax. We have to free ourselves from fear. Let ourselves just be.

The calmer our mind becomes, the clearer it becomes. It is like observing a glass of freshly-collected, but dirty, river water. If it is left alone, the sediment settles and the water becomes visibly clearer. Then we can observe the natural quality of cleanliness in the water. It is the same with the mind and how its true nature can be revealed. The nature of our mind is clean, like the undisturbed water. Peaceful, undisturbed, fresh, bright and alert. Joyful.

We also find that the more peaceful we are, the kinder we are.

By contrast, if our mind is fixated and obsessed it can become small. Generally the unhappy mind is not aware of the world but is self-absorbed with problems. The happy person is bouncy and bubbly, taking in the whole world around them; more open, observant and often more creative. The more calm and clear our mind is, the more aware it is. We allow ourselves to have a pristine awareness without grasping or clinging.

Our true nature is our natural state – it cannot be forced. Just relax. Let things come and go. We don't need to follow any thoughts or emotions that arise or force them to go away. We just observe them and let them be. If we don't feed them, then we often find they just disappear of their own accord.

A Buddhist guide to boredom

When we relax, we just sit and relax, doing almost nothing. Meditation is not about doing, it is about doing nothing. We might think it must be the most boring thing to do. But it is not boring, because boring is something.

Actually I never used to know what 'boring' meant, but I know now. People talk about it all the time. I went to America one time and had a very nice life whilst teaching there. They gave me a big television, not much work, and a nice flat. The television had about 100 channels. So, I sat down with my remote control, going up: 1,2,3,4 channels. And then going down the channels. After about two days of doing this, I suddenly realised: 'this is boredom – THIS is boredom'.

I consider learning about boredom a good experience: it is a kind of very active dissatisfaction. There is a tension: a kind of expectation to be entertained but at the same time not getting what you want. So I really discovered boredom experientially. I don't know whether I've experienced happiness or peace of mind. But I've definitely, really, deeply, experienced boredom!

I'm mentioning boredom here for a reason. It is not necessary to be bored, but boredom can come up when we are relaxing. We can be very bored by meditating if we expect something to happen very quickly: 'I'm doing meditation now. Is it happening yet? Why is it not happening? It should be happening!'. But that's not what we need to do. We need to learn that meditation is not about getting something. That's why people often say: 'Don't expect results'. But if you don't expect results, why do it at all?

I didn't really understand this before. I thought if we don't expect results, why do we do it? We usually do something because we think something is going to happen, or should happen, as a result. If nothing is going to happen, or we don't expect anything to happen, why should we do it at all?

But then, after a long time, after many years, I understood. It is not that we don't have a goal, of course we have a goal, otherwise why do it? But, if we approach it expecting something, we create a kind of tension. Looking forward and anticipating an experience, whether it is peaceful or not, is not meditation. It is just looking forward. Impatiently waiting, we might call it. That's not meditation. Then what is meditation?

Meditation is relaxing. That is why we say: 'Don't expect'. Because if we expect something to happen from meditating, it is not going to happen because we are not meditating. This is one of the most important things.

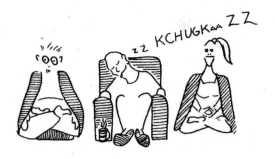

HUGH RELAXES TOO MUCH.

So we don't practise in this way. We are not looking forward to something and impatiently waiting for a result. Instead, we just relax, and whatever is happening, whatever experience is coming, whatever sensation is coming, whatever perceptions we have from the senses – we're open to them. We're not trying to stop our thoughts, we're not trying to change our perception, we're not trying to do anything. We're just open and relaxed.

The art of letting go... without pushing away

Whatever happens, if a sensation comes, a thought comes, perception comes, emotion comes – it is all okay. We just let it come, and let it be. If we say 'let it go', people can sometimes tend to try to push it away: 'Ah! Now it has come, I must get rid of it'. Then it is not letting go, it is actively pushing it away. Then it becomes like the same thing as before:

reacting with aversion, which is the same as running after and running away.

Pushing away is just running away – aversion. It is not meditation, it is just our usual way of reacting. Whatever is happening, good things, bad things, negative things, even the worst kind of disturbed thoughts, emotions and sensations – it just doesn't matter. It is okay. Let it come and let it be.

If we can practically learn how to do that then we will get some kind of confidence. We will accept that it is okay for thoughts, sensations and perceptions to come. They come, they go and something else comes and then something else comes, and so on. If we can manage to have this attitude, even if it is just for a short time, we are okay. It can come, it can go and it doesn't matter.

When we can say that any good or bad thing, any negative or positive thing, many or few things, can all arise in our mind, and it doesn't matter or make us suffer, and we don't have to run after or run away, then we have peace.

When we have peace in the mind, joy is the natural product. The more peaceful we are, the more joyful we become – because there's nothing disturbing us. There's no struggling and no fighting. We are peaceful, we are joyful and the more we become confident and gain certainty of this experience, the more joyful we become.

The joy arises because we learn how to deal with the manifestations of the mind, how to experience things. It is very subtle, and actually very simple in a way. It is nothing too complicated, it is not that we have to do anything very strange.

Sometimes people think that meditation is very mystical, some strange exercise, something mysterious. It is actually a way we can change our way of experiencing from within. If we can learn how to do that, we really can stabilise our mind.

Freedom from fear

In stabilising our mind, it is not that we have no more thoughts, no more emotions. It is not like that. It is that we learn how to deal with them, how to let these things come and go without becoming overpowered by them or taken over by them. And when we can say that any kinds of feelings, emotions, perceptions or thoughts are all okay, then we no longer have any fear.

This fearlessness is a deep kind. It is not about boasting of being strong and brave. Rather, it is a deep kind of fearlessness where we know how to deal with things. Whatever arises – it is okay. That experience then gives real satisfaction, happiness, joy and certainty. The certainty of knowing we can deal with anything.

It is not immediate. But slowly, slowly we become more and more certain, more and more confident. Then, when we become confident and completely certain about that, and know exactly and completely that we have mastered it, then we know there is nothing we need to do about ourselves. We are okay. There's nothing more we need to do for ourselves.

We call it *'liberation from within,'* because we've learned how to be natural, how to experience ourselves. We are aware of our true nature.

To expect progress to be fast is unrealistic. Our present state of mind is a kind of addiction. And, even if we have a relatively small addiction, for example if we have been smoking cigarettes for a few years, it is difficult to get rid of. The mind poisons of our present state of mind are an addiction and our habitual tendencies have been with us for even longer, for an immeasurable time.

So we have to be prepared to work gradually. And it is important to say that if we make something a burden we're likely to put it down, or drop it, sooner or later. This goes for practice too. I am my practice. Buddhism is a tool to learn how to practise.

Happy, yet?

Should we expect our practice to be joyful and happy? Again, the trick is not to get too expectant of, or attached to, 'joy'. Joy comes from peace of mind. It is naturally there when the mind is not agitated. The mind agitates if we run towards or away from things. So we only need to relax. It is not useful to run after or away from things too much. We've been doing that all our lives – and it is no more than running towards the end of a rainbow.

So we just do whatever we can. If whatever we want happens, good. If it doesn't, also good. Just relax. Even if we are very busy we can still relax. With a little bit of peace in the mind, and without tension, there can be more and more joy and kindness.

It can seem that in Buddhism we talk about suffering so much that sometimes people think 'Oh, Buddhism is obsessed with suffering'. I've heard this said very often. I visited a school in the UK, where the children studied religion and they were looking at Buddhism. The subject was the Four Noble Truths and the only thing they said was: 'Buddhists think that everything is suffering'. That was it!

So sometimes people have this gloomy expectation that everybody in Tibetan Buddhist monasteries will be silent, sad, serious and focusing on suffering. Then they go to one. They find the monks are naughty! They are not focusing on suffering at all, but on making jokes and playing pranks. In fact, sometimes it is a little hard for people from outside to visit, because the monks are always teasing and playing jokes.

I think that it is a misunderstanding that Buddhism is about suffering. It is not talking about suffering as much as talking about how to end suffering. So, we are really talking about happiness, not elated happiness or excitement, more of a peaceful joy. This is something that is very important. Buddhism as a teaching is not focused on anything else. It is not focused on the origin of beings. It is not focused on God or some higher power. It is totally focused on people, and all beings. How we can be better, deal with our problems, suffering and pain effectively, and how we can be completely happy?

From the spiritual point of view, if we learn how to change our way of experiencing, our attitudes and our way of perceiving, then we can be happy, joyful and satisfied whatever happens.

Realising wisdom: emptiness and interdependence

In the first chapter we discussed emptiness as one of the three qualities of the true nature of mind. The word *'emptiness'* was used by the Buddha, because we have such a strong tendency to see things as solid or real. So to counteract that, he talked of emptiness as a kind of 'shock treatment' for our pre-conceived assumptions. But we can just as easily misunderstand the word *'emptiness'*.

The term the Buddha used was *'shunyata'* which is generally translated as *'emptiness'*, but it might be better translated as *'interdependence'* or *'dependent arising'*. Many words are used to describe it, in fact, but they all come to the same point. [The relationship between emptiness and interdependence is discussed in the Heart Wisdom Series book *'Like Dreams & Clouds'*].

Nothing is completely independent. Everything is dependent on some other factor. That is the essence of interdependence. But even when we say this, it is still a little bit of a concept: 'Yes, it is all emptiness.' A label, with our mind conceptualising and imposing an idea. That could go wrong. It will not lead us to wisdom if it remains only a concept.

'*Emptiness*' could become misunderstood as ruling everything out or as nihilistic negation. If we see things as existing, that's okay. But if we have a nihilistic viewpoint, it is said that it is almost impossible to cure. They say that if it is misunderstood, *shunyata* is medicine turned into poison.

But if we see interdependence in a clear way it becomes wisdom. It allows us to understand exactly what we are. We have wisdom, and can free ourselves. We learn how to self-liberate. We see the true nature of mind. We don't just say 'Oh, the nature of my mind is emptiness'! But we actually see very clearly how interdependence works.

With practise, we learn how to self-liberate our thoughts and emotions. Thoughts, emotions and experiences arise in the mind. If we see their nature, we don't become a slave to them. We see the manifestations as waves in the ocean of mind, but we are not controlled and affected by them.

In our usual way of reacting at the moment, everything we experience leads us to react with aversion and attachment. If we see that we don't have to react with aversion or attachment, we know that's its all okay. Then we don't need to run after or run away. When our mind is free from fear, there is no need to suffer.

Wisdom can be experienced if we understand the true nature of mind as *emptiness* with *clarity* and *continuous flowing*. The more wisdom we have, the freer we are and the less we need to suffer.

Wisdom and compassion

When there is wisdom, there is compassion. The more we are free from reacting dualistically, then the more we don't have to look after the fake identity of 'me'. We then become concerned about others. Compassion for others develops as we realise we don't need to maintain our fake identity. So, our attention towards others develops – compassion grows – and we become less self-centred and selfish.

We don't have to be self-centred. There is no need to be selfish. Wisdom helps us to see this and so, directly, generates compassion. Compassion is a by-product of wisdom. Where there is wisdom, there has to be compassion. If there is no compassion, it can't be wisdom. It has to be something else.

I DON'T KNOW
WHAT YOU'VE GOT
THERE,
    BUT IT AIN'T
        WISDOM.

Wisdom is not necessarily an intellectual thing. Analysis can help to generate wisdom, for example reasoning 'it is not like this or that' and so on. But wisdom is not purely conceptual. Wisdom has to be inside. *Experienced.*

When you experience wisdom, it is just clearly seeing for yourself, opening your heart. Opening your eyes. Seeing clearly. So, therefore, wisdom is not just a concept. Wisdom is very similar to compassion: opening the heart and mind and becoming completely aware.

We sometimes describe it as co-emergent wisdom: a state of pristine awareness where there is no grasping, but great clarity. Where we are completely aware, but we don't need to hold onto anything. We are not limited by contrived distinctions: 'this is me' and 'this is my object of awareness'. We free ourselves from grasping too much. Grasping is what makes us suffer. Compassion, pure benevolence, is opening up without grasping. *Not* grasping at ourselves or at thoughts and emotions, the manifestations of the mind; that non-grasping brings wisdom. The more we become clear, the more wisdom arises naturally.

Our true nature has nothing wrong with it. It is only obscured by the defilements of our negative emotions (mind poisons or *kleshas*), our ignorance and habitual tendencies. Through compassion we purify our negative emotions and our negative way of reacting. The more our negative emotions and habits are cleared, the more we experience ourselves as we really are. Directly and indirectly, compassion works to bring wisdom. Awareness, without self-grasping to a 'me' or our false sense of a solid, independent self, is wisdom.

Discussion

Questioner: You explained the true nature of mind in three ways: that its essence is empty and that its nature is clarity with continual flow. Could you tell us how we actually experience it in our everyday life, in an unenlightened state?

Rinpoche: We just look at it. We analyse. Really look into where your mind is. Find out what your mind looks like. Where is it? Can you find it? You cannot pin it down. That is emptiness. But still you feel it! You can still experience with your mind. We can know the true nature of thoughts to be manifestations of the mind and recognise their nature as empty, but they still manifest. Manifestations of mind do not stop, even while you recognise that emptiness is a quality of the true nature of mind.

Questioner: Are thoughts an aspect of clarity?

Rinpoche: Yes. And the thoughts don't cease, they go on, the feelings go on, everything goes on, it does not stop. When you look, there is no mind anywhere, but still the thoughts arise. That is how you can understand it from a non-enlightened point or view, more or less. But when you're enlightened – then you see it very clearly.

Questioner: Can you explain a little bit more about the continual flow or unimpededness?

Rinpoche: In everyday life it is what we are thinking right now. Would your mind just completely STOP at any moment? No. That is the unimpededness. Would you stop having thoughts, emotions or other manifestations? Although you can't find it – its nature is clear – its function never stops. Our true nature is just like that.

Questioner: You explained about attachment and aversion. I understand that the underlying attachment is part of the basic ignorance, and is common to all the mind poisons, to all the kleshas, as is aversion. Is that correct?

Rinpoche: That is true – all the three are so interlinked, in a subtle way, that one cannot exist without the other. For instance if the ignorance was not there, you could not have the other two, the attachment and aversion.

Questioner: You have taught how suffering results from the habitual and dualistic way in which we misinterpret our mind's thoughts and emotions. But how can people learn about these manifestations if they are physically suffering, for example, from hunger? What then?

Rinpoche: Hunger is a very strong sensation. If someone is hungry, the best thing might just be to have something to eat. If you are very hungry, and say instead, 'Okay, now I will meditate and just let the hunger go', it doesn't quite happen! You can't do it just like that, on the spur of the moment, without any practice. Some people can be near-death and still be happy, but we can't just jump to work with extreme situations like that immediately. The path is a step-by-step process. Any training is a step-by-step process: first working on small things.

Initially it is best to have a nice situation or pleasant environment that isn't too challenging; ideally without too much noise or disturbance. Then we can learn how to practise meditation. We observe the thoughts and emotions that come. Gradually we learn how to let them come and go.

Then, if we are able to practise meditation with stability in that situation, we might attempt to practise within a slightly less favourable environment. We could try to do it in the course of our normal day or when we are in a working situation. We could see how it goes. If you find that it is also possible to do that, then you can keep on doing it. Then, eventually, maybe sometimes you can do it even in very intense and very severe situations. It is possible for people experiencing severe sickness, and sometimes even dying, to still be happy. There have been many people who have managed this. It's possible if we are really good at meditating. But we can't just jump immediately into doing that, I don't think that is possible. It is a step-by-step thing.

Questioner: It seems that there is a process of learning to open up to our true nature. Does it have to do with an 'unlearning' of things?

Rinpoche: Yes, you can say that if you like – we are 'unlearning' the habitual ways we react, but it is more like becoming natural. It's more learning how to be natural. So you can say it is unlearning if you like – it comes to the same thing, I think.

But, if we do use the word 'learn' - it is not about 'getting information'. When I say 'learning' it is not about getting lots of information and then becoming very sophisticated and detailed. Sometimes people understand 'learning' like that, for example, 'I have to learn about this flower so I'm going to analyse it in segments. This has three things. This has four things. This has five things. This has six things. This has seven things.' Not that kind of learning.

It's more of an unfolding, so you can say that if you like, an unfolding. The spiritual way of learning is more about going inward. You take away one level, the next level you also take out and so on, until you discover what is inside, at the root. That is more the spiritual way of learning: it is an uncovering or discovering.

Questioner: Is part of opening up to our true nature developing acceptance of the natural emotions we have?

Rinpoche: Yes, it is and it is very important to understand this. You don't become insensitive; you become sensitive. The main understanding is that we work on emotions to be able to liberate our emotions. It's not that you block the emotions, and it is not that you don't block the emotions either. Instead, you understand deeply that there's no need to feel like that, so therefore you don't react in that way.

I always give this example. If I hear that something happened that makes me very sad, or very angry, for instance, then I have a very sad or angry emotion. But then if, after some time, I find out that it never happened at all like that, if I find out very clearly that the cause for which I felt this emotion never happened, then what happens to my emotion? It just dissolves, because it is not needed any more. If I was angry, I am not angry at all now. I don't have to block it or do anything, it is just not there any more. It is the same with the sadness or whatever other emotion arose. Why? Because there is no need, no necessity, no reason to have this emotion. So, therefore, it just goes away.

So, that is how to deal with any emotion in the same way. You understand deeply that it is not necessary to react like that. There is no use; there is no benefit; there is no need to react like that, because it doesn't help you. It doesn't help anyone. When we deeply understand this, then that emotion just disappears. We don't have to hold on to it, and we don't have to fight against it. Because it just dissolves. We deeply, experientially understand that there is no need to hold onto it. That's the most important thing.

Questioner: But if somebody we really love is going through a painful experience, we naturally respond with a sense of sadness, that the person is experiencing suffering or pain.

Rinpoche: Yes, of course, if something sad happens, you feel sadness. When we speak of learning how to deal with emotions, it is not that you become insensitive. You become more sensitive in a way, very clearly sensitive. So therefore, when something sad happens, yes, you feel sad. But we don't hold on to that sadness for a long time. We can let it go, that's the main thing. Because we realise that it is not useful to hold on to the sadness for a long time. We realise that we don't need to; and that it doesn't help others or ourselves to keep on being sad. Of course we can try to help, we try to do whatever we can, but we don't hold on to the sadness. We learn how to let these emotions come and go. So we can be sad sometimes, but we don't have to be continuously sad.

Questioner: Is compassion beyond emotional states such as sadness?

Rinpoche: Yes, compassion is not about my feelings; it is about others. Compassion is about others. Feeling sad, feeling angry or feeling anxious and things like that, is all about me and my reactions. But compassion is for others, and it is not necessary to be sad. We can say, 'This should not happen. It is causing suffering and problems for others.' So we really want things to change. Then if we are motivated or inspired to improve something through compassion, we should do it.

Questioner: Following on from that – is there ever a manifestation of mind (either a memory, emotion or thought) that we shouldn't apply mindfulness to? One that is either so extreme or of such a nature that we should actively fight against it? Or is mindfulness a universal antidote to all contents of consciousness?

Rinpoche: We work on our emotions because we don't want to suffer and we don't want to have problems. So we learn ways to work on ourselves. That's why we do it. That doesn't mean that you should not fight for justice, and act to make things change for the better. That's another thing that we have to do – and that is what we call compassion.

Usually we say, from a Buddhist point of view, that anger and compassion come from the same situation, and I think that is very important. Something happens that we feel should not happen. Maybe we see that is happening. But then, if we concentrate on 'the people who did this' or 'the person who did this' and the subsequent conclusion that they are very bad, then we will just get angry. Because it becomes personal.

But, if we concentrate on the issue, and our focus goes to the issue, then it becomes compassion. Because then it is not about fighting against a person or people, or how you're feeling about it. Instead, it becomes about how to solve the situation. 'This situation is not a good thing, it should be solved. It is not beneficial, it is harmful for many people ... so how can I solve this problem?'. That is compassionate. That way, we are not feeling angry or generating bad feelings against somebody. Rather, we just want to solve the problem. That's compassion.

Questioner: You mentioned *shiné* meditation as a method for calming the mind. At what stage can we move on to practising insight meditation to help realise wisdom?

Rinpoche: It isn't that you cannot practice insight meditation (called *vipassana* in Sanskrit or *lhaktong* in Tibetan) until your calm-abiding meditation (*shamatha* in Sanskrit or *shiné* in Tibetan) is very stable; but the more stable our *shamatha* is, the better our *vipassana* will be.

But you needn't wait until you are a great *shamatha* meditator. We need both.

Sometimes, for some people, for various reasons, *shamatha* is very easy. Sometimes, for others it is very difficult. But that doesn't necessarily mean they will not have any *vipassana* experience.

Actually, they are not two things. *Shamatha* can be with insight – then it is *vipassana*. *Vipassana* could be a very good method for bringing *shamatha*. The more we see the nature of mind, the more we understand the way things are, the more we are able to relax.

If we are able to see that things are not so solid, that our thoughts and emotions are not that solid, then we are able to deal with them more easily. We are able to let them come and go and we are able to relax a little bit more. If we analyse the nature of thoughts and emotions, that can help bring more a stable *vipassana*. It is always taught that *shamatha* and *vipassana* go together and support each other. Hand in hand.

All my babbling,
In the name of Dharma
Has been set down faithfully
By my dear students of pure vision.

I pray that at least a fraction of the wisdom
Of those enlightened teachers
Who tirelessly trained me
Shines through this mass of incoherence.

May the sincere efforts of all those
Who have worked tirelessly
Result in spreading the true meaning of Dharma
To all who are inspired to know.

May this help dispel the darkness of ignorance
In the minds of all living beings
And lead them to complete realisation
Free from all fear.

Ringu Tulku

Acknowledgements

Conrad Harvey dedicates his editorial work on this text to Elliot Jetsun and Oakley Sherab, for when they are older; and thanks Jonathan Clewley, Mary Heneghan, Maria Hundörf-Kaiser, Carole McMeckan, Ngedon George and Uma Naomi Harvey, and Rebecca and Paul O'Connor for their invaluable assistance.

About the Author

Ringu Tulku Rinpoche is a Tibetan Buddhist Master of the Kagyu Order. He was trained in all schools of Tibetan Buddhism under many great masters including HH the 16th Gyalwang Karmapa and HH Dilgo Khyentse Rinpoche. He took his formal education at Namgyal Institute of Tibetology, Sikkim and Sampurnananda Sanskrit University, Varanasi, India. He served as Tibetan Textbook Writer and Professor of Tibetan Studies in Sikkim for 25 years.

Since 1990, he has been travelling and teaching Buddhism and meditation in Europe, America, Canada, Australia and Asia. He participates in various interfaith and 'Science and Buddhism' dialogues and is the author of several books on Buddhist topics. These include Path to Buddhahood, Daring Steps, The Ri-me Philosophy of Jamgon Kongtrul the

Great, Confusion Arises as Wisdom, the Lazy Lama series and the Heart Wisdom series, as well as several children's books, available in Tibetan and European languages.

He founded the organisations:
Bodhicharya - see www.bodhicharya.org
and Rigul Trust - see www.rigultrust.org

Other books by Bodhicharya Publications

The Lazy Lama Series:

No. 1 - Buddhist Meditation

No. 2 - The Four Noble Truths

No. 3 - Refuge: Finding a Purpose and a Path

No. 4 - Bodhichitta: Awakening Compassion and Wisdom

No. 5 - Living without Fear and Anger

No. 6 - Relaxing in Natural Awareness

Heart Wisdom Series:

The Ngöndro: *Foundation Practices of Mahamudra*

From Milk to Yoghurt: *A Recipe for Living and Dying*

Like Dreams and Clouds: *Emptiness and Interdependence; Mahamudra and Dzogchen*

Dealing with Emotions: *Scattering the Clouds*

Journey from Head to Heart: *Along a Buddhist Path*

See: www.bodhicharya.org/publications

Rigul TrusT

Patron: Ringu Tulku Rinpoche

Rigul Trust is a UK charity whose objectives are the relief of poverty and financial hardship, the advancement of education, the advancement of religion, the relief of sickness, the preservation of good health.

Our main project is helping with health and education in Rigul, Tibet, the homeland of Ringu Tulku Rinpoche where his monastery is. We currently fund Dr Chuga, the nurse, the doctor's assistant, the running costs of the health clinic, the teachers, the cooks and the children's education plus two, free, hot meals a day at school.

We also help raise funds for disasters like earthquakes, floods, and help with schools in India and other health and welfare projects. All administration costs are met privately by volunteers.

100% OF ALL DONATIONS GOES TO FUND HEALTH, EDUCATION AND POVERTY RELIEF PROJECTS

Rigul Trust

13 St. Francis Avenue, Southampton, SO18 5QL U.K.

info@rigultrust.org

UK Charity Registration No: 1124076

TO FIND OUT MORE, OR MAKE A DONATION, PLEASE VISIT:

www.rigultrust.org

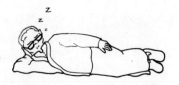

For an up to date list of books by Ringu Tulku,
please see the Books section at

www.bodhicharya.org

*All proceeds received by Bodhicharya Publications
from the sale of this book go direct to humanitarian
and educational projects because the work involved in
producing this book has been given free of charge.*